Pineal Gland & Your Third Eye

Proven Methods to Develop Your HIGHER SELF

Soft Cover Edition
September 2014

By

Dr. Jill Ammon-Wexler
http://www.BuildMindPower.com

Dr. Jill Ammon-Wexler

Copyright © 2011-2014 by Jill Ammon-Wexler. All international rights reserved. This book is presented as educational material and is not meant to replace the support of your personal medical, alternate health specialist, psychologist, spiritual advisor or counselor. Neither the publisher nor the author accepts any liability for the misuse of this educational information.

ISBN:099103791X
ISBN:13: 9780991037919
Quantum Self Group Inc., Sandpoint, Idaho, USA

Soft Cover Edition Published by
Quantum Self Group, Inc.
217 Cedar Street #268,
Sandpoint, Idaho 83864 USA

TOPICS

The **ANCIENT BELIEF** that we have a "third eye" dates thousands if years back, and is found in spiritual and metaphysical traditions from around the world. It is often referred to as the gateway leading into our inner realms of higher states of awareness and consciousness.

The **MYSTERIOUS PINEAL GLAND** connection to your "higher self" has been proven to have exact correlates in the brain. Discover what the research findings mean to YOU, and explore the pineal gland-third eye connection.

Use **16 DETAILED METHODS** to discover how-to activate your pineal gland to open your third eye – from acupressure to ancient chanting and visualization techniques long proven to work.

Experience exactly how a **THIRD EYE OPENING** feels on a sensory level as you watch this video.

Dr. Jill Ammon-Wexler

Understand your **MOTIVATION** as you explore an interesting concept of how our everyday motivation determines our level of consciousness, and what you can DO to immediately expand your consciousness.

LOOK INSIDE YOUR BRAIN to discover why the secret to developing access to your higher self is easily understood by learning a bit more about how your brain does what it does. This is a life changer.

Learn how to **GET STARTED** boosting your consciousness ... starting with you are today. Includes an easy way to clarify exactly where you are right now.

Build your **SELF-AWARENESS** by taking steps to identify exactly WHAT you can immediately do to increase your consciousness.

Determine if you are **PSYCHIC** as you review the scientific research suggesting you already DO have innate psychic abilities.

Use pages of **ADDITIONAL RESOURCES** and references to useful and interesting higher states research and tools, plus information on an available collection of audio-quality downloadable brainwave trainings.

CONTENTS

Forward - 7

One: A Brief History - 13

Two: Scientific Evidence - 21
The Pineal Gland
The "Opening" Experience
The Case of DMT
Psychedelics
Meditation and the Brain
Brain Training

Three: Opening the Third Eye -35
1. Acupressure
2. Brain Training
3. Chakra Stimulation
4. Chanting
5. Hypnosis & Visualization
6. Progressive Relaxation Method
7. Third Eye Mudra
8. Reflexology
9. Kundalini Energy

10. Tapping
11. Alternate Nostril Breathing
12. Third Eye Breathing
13. Yantra Meditation
14. Balasana Yoga Pose
15. Third Eye Visualization
16. Essential Oils

Four: Are You Psychic? - 69

Five: Awareness - 71

Six: Motivation & Higher States - 81

Seven: Self-Awareness - 87

Eight: Higher Intelligence - 95

Nine. The Speed of Thought - 99

Ten. Pineal Gland Health - 105

Eleven. RELATED RESOURCES - 111

Twelve. About The Author - 115

References - 117

FORWARD

"Knowing others is intelligence, knowing yourself is true wisdom. --The Tao Te Ching

Before we begin, allow me to reveal why I decided to write this book. I began my university education as a dedicated scientist. As a premedical student I spent long hours immersed in technical books and lab courses.

Psychology? That was my second "major," simply because I felt it might make me a better medical doctor; but science was my first love.

Then toward the end of my senior year, something totally unexpected happened. I "tagged along" with a friend to observe an unusual research project.

The project, a study of the brainwaves of meditators, was being conducted by an informal group of grad students from UC San Jose, Stanford and Berkeley. What I saw that day erased my goal of becoming a medical doctor – and ended up literally changing my life.

What could have been so dramatic? The magic of watching a thought create waves of energy graphed on an EEG captivated me.

I looked over the shoulders of a small group that was excitedly comparing the results from two different "subjects" – one an experienced meditator, and the other subject one of the researchers who had never meditated.

The source of their excitement was circled on one of the charts with a red felt tip marker. The excitement? The meditator's steady flow of Alpha brainwaves, vs. a few tiny bursts of Alpha in the non-meditator. They had captured scientific proof that meditation changes the brain.

That was in direct contrast with what was being taught medical students at the time. We were being told that the brain we are born with is unchangeable – including your IQ, your level of awareness, and most certainly your mental potential. Now it seemed that was not true.

On that day I developed a passion to decode how the brain and behavior work together. I turned away from medical school and enrolled in grad school with a major in psychology.

On weekends I then either went to the Big Sur to attend seminars at Esalen, or to Sausalito to join a small group of people visiting with Alan Watts on his houseboat.

My serious study of the sciences was replaced by passionate excitement and discovery as I rubbed shoulders with mystics, gurus, meditation teachers, Tibetan lamas, metaphysicians, amazing thought leaders, channels, and shaman. The whole world became alive with potential, and I could feel my own brain expanding to take it all in.

I moved from my flat near the university up into the redwood forested mountains behind Monterey Bay and began to renovate a tiny cabin. The vertical energy of the redwoods drew me even deeper into meditation and an impassioned study of higher states of consciousness.

Then one night my remaining skepticism about "higher states of awareness" was very seriously challenged. I was suddenly awakened by a bright light racing toward me through the window at the head of the bed.

When the beam of light hit the top of my head the force propelled me feet-first, covers and all, right off the end of the bed. My poor tomcat, who had been sleeping by my feet, suffered a broken tail.

The next day I hiked to one of my favorite spots by the river and laid on my back looking up into the redwood canopy. I was watching a tiny spider drop from the top of one of the redwoods, spinning a single silver strand as it descended.

Then in the next instant I realized how remarkable it was to be able to see that, the sound of loud pop in the back of my head changed everything yet again.

I could clearly see that tiny spider in bold detail from at least 30 feet down. The trees were breathing and the river was singing. My third eye had popped opened!

All this while I was also serving in a very serious capacity as the mind power resource to a long list of corporate executives.

What happened? I found I was even more effective helping my clients resolve their issues due to an amazing increase in my intuitive abilities.

So, I can personally reassure you that taking steps to activate your third eye is most likely a direct path to increased self awareness, which in turn DOES lead to exciting higher states of consciousness and deeper meaning in your life.

This is an invitation to expand beyond your everyday reality, to experience higher states of conscious awareness. But whether or not you choose to actually work at opening your third eye, simply doing these exercises WILL directly improve your mind power.

Your innermost wisdom, intuition, psychic abilities, clairvoyance, higher consciousness, divine experiences and higher states of awareness are ALL directly related to your third eye.

This soft cover edition of this book takes you step-by-step through PROVEN methods you can use to activate your pineal gland and open your third eye – or to simply expand your consciousness and awareness, depending upon your personal goals.

The focus is on exercises you can use to consciously tap into YOUR higher self and reach new levels of consciousness. By "higher self" I am referring to that aspect of yourself that connects you to extraordinary mental states occurring outside of your everyday "ordinary" consciousness.

The concept there is part of you that transcends your ordinary conscious mind may seem questionable; but today's scientific evidence suggests we do indeed have access to a source of unlimited intelligence we can tap into through our own super-conscious mind and an open third eye.

In terms of modern quantum physics, the higher self IS you! The only reason I refer to "connecting" to it is because we've been trained from birth not to focus on that aspect of our being. So what IS your higher self?

It is the very highest and best you're capable of being and expressing. And opening your third eye puts you in direct contact with this wonderful, totally natural aspect of yourself.

Enjoy the journey!

Dr Jill Ammon-Wexler

ONE: A BRIEF HISTORY

The belief we have a "higher self" we can access through a "third eye" goes far, far back into history. Mystery schools once flourished throughout the ancient civilizations of Greece, Egypt, India, China and South America.

These secret teaching centers guided students through a metaphysical education that included a series of "wisdom trials" and initiations designed to open them to higher states of awareness and consciousness.

In a fascinating book entitled "Mystic Americanism," author Grace Morey explained that "The All-Seeing Eye – symbolic of the pineal gland or third eye – has been found amid the ruins of almost every civilization upon the globe."

These ancient schools were actually universities of the higher self. The shared goal of these ancient mystery schools was the conscious realization that we are each directly connected to the one universal source of life.

Interestingly, this same concept of our connection to universal source of consciousness in now supported by many findings of the sciences of modern Field Theory, String Theory and Quantum Physics.

Ancient Egypt

For more than 3,000 years the mystery schools of Egypt epitomized the ultimate in secret wisdom and knowledge. In ancient Egypt the third eye was portrayed as the eye of Horus, or Ra.

Many modern scholars and researchers theorize that the great teachers of the Egyptian mystery schools had to originate from some unknown extraordinary place.

Some believe advanced teachers survived the destruction of an ancient civilization and made their way to Egypt, where they elevated it to a level of greatness far in advance of other cultures of the day.

Buddhism

In Buddhism, the third eye is a well-known symbol of a higher state of consciousness and enlightenment. Most educated people from around the world are familiar with the symbol of the Buddha, with both the third eye and crown chakra clearly portrayed.

Channeling

Channeling, the process of receiving information or inspiration said to flow from dimensions beyond our normally perceived physical reality, is commonly believed to be connected to an active third eye.

Where does the channeled information or inspiration originate from? You may have encountered people who feel they are channeling spirit guides, angels, extraterrestrials and ascended masters.

Could channeling come from an ability to simply connect to one's higher level of consciousness through an activated pineal gland? Possibly!

Whatever the source, the channeling process can only be as clear as the individual "channel." To achieve the required levels of mental clarity, most people commit to a journey of personal growth to learn to consciously enter into higher states of consciousness – including efforts to activate their third eye.

Hinduism

In the East Indian tradition, the third eye is referred to as the gyananakash – "the eye of knowledge." It is also referred to as the antar-guru – the seat of the "teacher inside."

The ancient Upanishads likened a human being to a city with ten gates. Nine gates (eyes, nostrils, ears, mouth, etc.) lead outside to the sensory world.

The third eye is the tenth gate, and was said to lead to inner spaces of higher consciousness.

The "Encyclopedic Dictionary of Yoga" states that the third eye "Ajna Chakra" is connected with the sacred syllable Om, and that after activation of this center the aspirant overcomes their ego – the last hurdle on the Hindu path of spirituality.

According to Hinduism, the third eye chakra is also the exit point for one's kundalini energy. Hindu men and women often apply marks to their foreheads intended to retain their kundalini energy, and to strengthen and protect their third eye focus and concentration.

The tilak (from the Sanskrit "tilaka, or "mark") is often seen on the foreheads of Hindu men. The tilak consists of one or more lines, and often indicates the man's sectarian affiliation.

In addition to its religious symbolism, the tilak is also believed to have a cooling effect on the forehead said to aid third eye concentration and meditation.

A dot of red sandalwood paste, a bindi, is often applied between and just above the eyebrows of women in India, Bangladesh, Nepal, and Sri Lanka. In some of these cultures this may indicate a woman's marriage status, but it always also represents a form of protection for their third eye.

Kundalini Yoga

In the East, awakening the third eye (the ajna chakra) is often approached through the discipline of yoga, and especially Kundalini Yoga. In ancient Sanskrit, "kundalini" means "illumination" or "enlightenment," and refers to the internal light said to be experienced when you awaken your third eye.

PINEAL GLAND & YOUR THIRD EYE

The yogic tradition holds that the proper way to activate the third eye is to balance two opposite energy channels in the body (ida and pingala) around a central vertical axis of energy called the sushumna.

This balance of opposites creates a third force that unites the opposites and awakens the third eye, allowing you to see your true essence.

Achieving this balance is generally an experience that is conferred upon a seeker by a Kundalini Yoga master.

Freemasonry

Another image commonly believed to represent the third eye is common to various Western Secret

A Masonic Apron

Societies, and often appears in both Freemasonry and Rosicrucian symbols. Such a symbol is found, for example, on both modern and ancient Masonic temples and aprons, as shown in the preceding illustration.

Since the understanding of the third eye was forbidden during the intellectual intolerance of the Dark and Middle Ages, the secret societies of that time designed symbolic third eye symbols into the architectural facades of churches, castles and buildings around the world – often using a particular symbol of a rose (often present as a window) surrounded by two columns, as also portrayed on the previous picture of the Masonic apron.

Founders of the USA

Have you ever wondered about the "eye-in-the-triangle" positioned above a truncated pyramid on the back of the US $1 bill?

Some believe this could be a "salute" to the metaphysical Masonic fraternity that is still present worldwide.

There is also a thought that the early founders of America, some of who were known to be Freemasons, may have memorialized this same symbol on the "Great Seal" of the United States.

Hawaiian Huna

In the ancient Hawaiian Huna tradition, the symbol "Waha Hamama," meaning "to reveal secrets" or "the open mouth," is believed to be very powerful when meditated upon while focusing on your third eye.

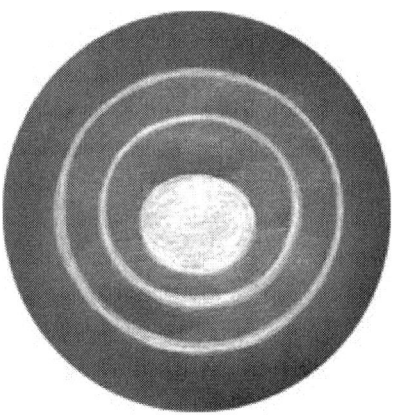

In the Huna of Kuauhaoali'i, Daddy Bray, Poppa Bray, and Taneo Sands Kumalae, this symbol is said to open

Dr. Jill Ammon-Wexler

up and reveal both mundane and meaningful secrets, and to reveal psychic visions and hearing things which are "subtle, hidden, or far distant."

This Hawaiian wisdom lineage believes this symbol to be highly effective when meditated upon in the 3rd eye. It is said to portray enlightenment into the secrets of the soul and why you are here.

Note: A resource of additional information on this and other ancient Huna symbols has been included in the Reference directory of this book.

Ancient Huna teachings were not openly discussed or written down, but have historically been passed from initiate to initiate from one generation to the next. The initiates are called kahuna, meaning the "Keepers of the Secret." Huna methods are often taught at the Nine Gates Mystery School in California. You can inquire here: http://www.ninegates.org/

New Age Spirituality

In modern New Age spirituality, the third eye symbolizes the state of enlightenment and also the evocation of mental images with deep personal spiritual or psychological meaning. The third eye is often associated with clairvoyance, ESP, visions, empathy, channeling, precognition, remote viewing, astral travel and out-of-body experiences.

TWO: SCIENTIFIC EVIDENCE

Modern science is now confirming what mystics and shaman have claimed for thousands and thousands of years – we have a "higher" aspect of our being, and it is directly connected to a dynamic source of conscious energy that is far more expansive than our individual selves.

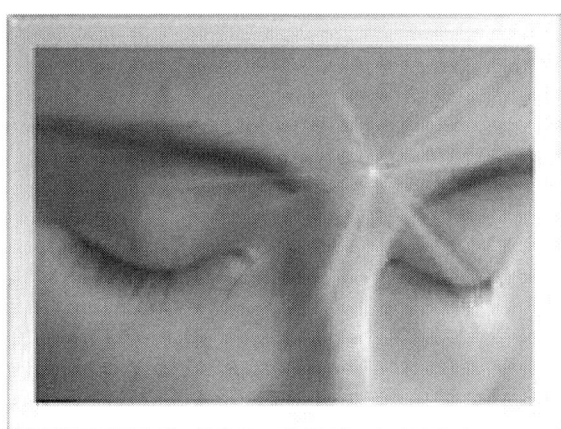

Did you realize that your body actually does have three physical eyes? The mysterious "third eye" has been long been pondered by mystics, who believe the "inner vision" of our third eye is our natural connection to a source of higher energy and consciousness.

The Pineal Gland

Let's take a closer look at your third eye. You may be surprised to learn that such a "third eye" actually DOES exist. It's a tiny gland in your brain – the pineal gland, also called the "epiphysis."

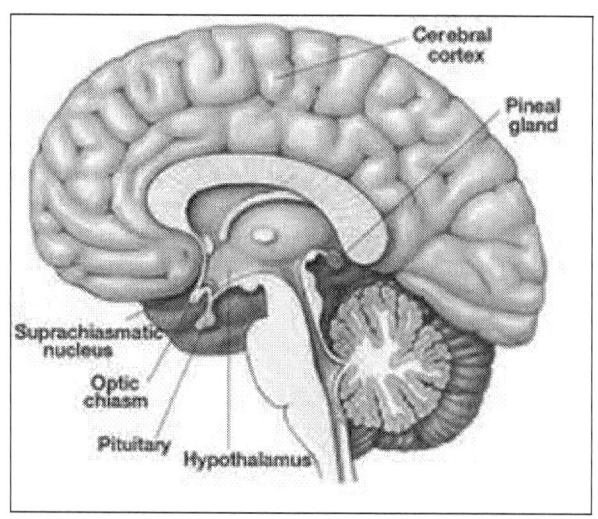

Your pineal gland is located in the exact geometric center of your brain, and is said to expand outward to the middle of your forehead when your third eye is opened.

Interestingly, many metaphysicians feel that the pineal gland's position in the center of the brain correlates to the location of the ancient Great Pyramid located in the center of planet Earth.

The pineal gland is about the size of a pea, and is located in a tiny cave behind and above the pituitary gland. It lies directly behind your eyes, and is attached to your brain's third ventricle.

The pineal gland has many characteristics of your two exterior eyes. It has a lens and contains a complete map of the visual field of the eyes. The pineal gland's pinealocytes photoreceptor cells are equivalent to the photoreceptor cells found in your eyes.

The pineal gland secretes melatonin when you are relaxed and visualizing, and also responds to electromagnetic energy. Interestingly, although this gland is deep inside your skull, it is directly activated by light, and manages to control your body's natural biorhythms.

Although the physical presence of the pineal gland was not confirmed until recently, mystical and esoteric traditions have long felt this tiny portion of our brain connects us to alternate realities and higher levels of consciousness.

The true function of this mysterious pineal gland was long contemplated by philosophers and spiritual adepts.

The ancient Greeks believed the pineal gland was a direct connection to the mysterious universal "Realms of Thought." The great philosopher Rene Descartes spent many years studying the pineal gland, and referred to it as the "Seat of the Soul."

In terms of modern science, it was asserted by Stephen Phillips in Extrasensory Perception of Quarks that the third eye's microscopic vision is actually capable of observing sub-atomic objects as small as quarks.

So then, what would "opening your third eye" be in more practical terms? Can we somehow stimulate our pineal gland to achieve an awareness of things not perceived by our natural senses? Or could it be like the experience occurring from a head injury or electro-convulsive treatment (ECT)?

The "Opening" Experience

How can you know if your third eye is open, or is at least in the process of opening? You may know your third eye is at least partially open if you tend to make accurate intuitive decisions and evaluations about your life, work, creativity, relationships and the intentions and emotions of other people.

You may often know things without being able to describe how you know them. You probably also have a very clear sense of personal direction, and a clear picture of where your life is headed.

You can assume that your third eye is still "under development" if you often feel a bit indecisive, lack commitment to your decisions, or may not have a clear sense of purpose for your life, although you wish to.

When you experience a third eye opening you may experience a vibration or pressure in your body, or hear a popping sound in the back of your head. Both of these sensations are perfectly normal.

Some people have an experience of entering into a tunnel radiating a beautiful purple or white light at the end.

Once you have connected with your third eye you may also feel a sense of floating in a sea of energy. Your mind will be flooded with light, insights, and inspiration. This may happen gradually over time, or quite suddenly.

Note: In my personal experience, third eye opening does not occur only once, but again and again over time.

I have especially noted the "popping sound" when I focus on healing, and a sense of vibration often accompanies this if I am administering a hands-on healing for myself. I can also tell you without a doubt that this is accompanied by unexpected brilliant insights and inspiration.

The Case of DMT

The pineal gland excretes dimethyltryptamine (DMT), a powerful and totally natural psychedelic known to induce dreams, near-death experiences, remote viewing, deep spiritual experiences, channeling, and out-of-body and shamanic-travel experiences.

DMT is also found naturally in several plants, and is the primary psychoactive in ayahuasca, a native Amazon tea used for higher insight and healing purposes.

Doctor Rick Strassman, a medical doctor who specializes in psychiatry, investigated the effects of dimethyltryptamine (DMT) extensively. Strassman is convinced that this powerful psychedelic could be naturally produced in the human pineal gland.

DMT has been found to be directly related to our brain's neurotransmitters, including serotonin, and the melatonin secreted by your pineal gland.

There's a lot of speculation about the role DMT plays while we are dreaming. It has been demonstrated that once you enter the rapid eye movement (REM) stage of sleep, minute amounts of this natural psychedelic are released directly into your bloodstream. This could help explain why some dreams can seem so "psychedelic."

Over the five-year duration of a major research project, Strassman administered an estimated 400 doses of DMT to 60 human volunteers.

He soon began to refer to DMT as the "god molecule" or "spirit molecule," because many of his research subjects said DMT brought them into direct contact with metaphysical beings, or even what they interpreted as being God.

His research was conducted in Albuquerque, New Mexico, where he was serving at that time as an Associate Professor of Psychiatry.

Doctor Strassman has also noted that DMT is first produced by the human fetus on the forty-ninth day of development– the exact point of life said by Buddhism to mark the "beginning of the soul." He has since also conducted similar research using psilocybin, a natural psychedelic found in hallucinogenic mushrooms.

Psychedelics

For thousands of years, many cultures have ingested both natural and manufactured concoctions with the goal of altering the user's state of consciousness. Many scientific studies of such substances have been conducted.

In 2006 the US government funded a Johns Hopkins University study of the spiritual effects of psilocybin. Psilocybin is a plant alkaloid that affects the brain's serotonin system, and in particular affects the 5-HT2A receptor.

The study involved 36 college-educated adults (average age of 46) who had never tried psilocybin. The subjects said they did not have a history of drug use, but did have religious or spiritual interests. The participants were closely observed for eight-hour intervals in a laboratory while under the influence of psilocybin.

This highly reputable study concluded that the active ingredient in hallucinogenic mushrooms (psilocybin) seems to produce a "higher states" experience with lasting positive effects.

A psilocybin mushroom

One-third of the participants stated that the experience was the single most spiritually significant moment of their lives, and more than two-thirds reported it was among their top five most spiritually significant experiences.

Some reported a sense of being able to "see beyond the physical appearances" of their environment.

Two months after the study, 79% of the participants still reported increased well-being or satisfaction – friends, relatives, and associates confirmed this. They also reported anxiety and depression symptoms were decreased, or completely gone.

"Under very defined conditions, and with careful preparation, you can safely and fairly reliably experience a mystical experience that may lead to positive changes," said study leader Professor Roland Griffiths.

Ian McGregor, a professor of psychopharmacology at the University of Sydney in Australia, says he isn't surprised that this study confirms the ability of psilocybin to induce a spiritual state. "Psilocybin and related hallucinogens have been used since ancient times in religious rituals ... and this study is really formalizing what many people already know, [but] to see a positive effect two months later is quite striking," he concludes.

Professor David Nichols of the Purdue University School of Pharmacy feels it's likely that psilocybin triggers the same neurological process that produces religious experiences during fasting, meditation, third eye opening, out-of-body experiences, sleep deprivation and near-death experiences (NDEs). "Psilocybin can occasion mystical-type experiences

having substantial and sustained personal meaning and spiritual significance," Nichols says.

Meditation and the Brain

Over 45 years of research and investigation have produced evidence of something meditators have claimed for centuries – meditation physically changes the brain, allowing long-term meditators to achieve remarkable levels of awareness and consciousness.

The Tibetans have a centuries-old tradition of intensive meditation, and the Dalai Lama was interested in having a scientific researcher scientifically explore the monks' meditating minds.

A few years back the Dalai Lama set up a study with neuroscientist Dr. Richard Davidson of the University of Wisconsin at Madison, who was already convinced from his research that meditation definitely produces changes in the brain.

Davidson used an EEG to study the brain's electrical activity of the Tibetan monks as they alternated between periods of meditation and a neutral state. The monks had been trained in the Tibetan Nyingmapa and Kagyupa traditions for an estimated 10,000 to 50,000 hours over periods of from 15 to 40 years.

As a control Davidson used 10 student volunteers with no previous meditation experience, but who were taught a simple meditation technique they practiced for one week.

As the Tibetan monks shifted from a neutral state to a meditative state they showed "a very sharp transition to prolonged periods of high-amplitude, synchronized oscillations in the Gamma (brainwave) frequency range," Davidson reported.

Davidson also found that the movement of the brainwaves through the brain was significantly more organized and coordinated than in the control group.

Some of the monks produced Gamma wave activity more powerful than any previously reported in a healthy person, Davidson explained.

He now explains these meditative higher states experiences as "high-frequency Gamma brainwaves and accompanying brain synchrony" (hemispheric balance). "Long-time practitioners (meditators) show brain activation on a scale we have never seen before," Davidson says. "Their mental practice demonstrates that the brain is capable of being trained and physically modified in ways few people can imagine."

Note: One way to teach your brain to duplicate this high Gamma "hemispheric balance brain synchrony" brainwave state is through the use of the "Whole Brain Sync" MP3 in the audio collection described in the Appendix section of this book.

The intense Gamma brainwaves and brain synchrony Davidson found in the meditating monks has also been associated with higher mental states, third eye activation, and dramatically heightened states of consciousness and awareness.

Brain Training

The initial research of the brains of meditators has created a booming interest in the use of brainwave training to create altered states of consciousness.

Brainwave training is based on the natural tendency of our brain to "follow along" with a regular beat, such as the way we tap our foot to keep time with music.

At brainwave frequencies of deep Theta and high Delta, the sense of your ordinary ego boundary often vanishes. You become less concerned with your normal "physical" existence, and more connected to higher states of consciousness and awareness.

According to many ancient traditions, this is when your third eye begins to activate and exhibit its special powers.

Dr. Jill Ammon-Wexler

THREE: OPENING THE THIRD EYE

There are many approaches to opening your third eye. The most popular methods are explored in the following pages, along with a series of proven-effective exercises for your use.

Although I have personally tested and used all of the methods detailed in the following pages, I have also included specific references to others who also recommend these same approaches so you can continue your research.

According to ancient traditions, our third eye is the gateway or portal to space and time. The pineal gland is then said to activate as the third eye link directly into higher states of consciousness.

Interestingly, the bony plates directly in front of the third eye reportedly tend to become thinner in long-time meditators and serious "seekers."

Dr. Jill Ammon-Wexler

1. Acupressure

It's said that Sigmund Freud used a touch procedure to help his patients access information they didn't seem to know consciously.

Freud would place his index finger on his patient's face between their eyebrows, apply a bit of pressure, and ask them to think of what they needed to know. He told them that when he removed his finger, they would suddenly remember what had been hidden away.

Reportedly this worked! It seems Freud was using a simple acupressure technique by pressing on his patient's third eye forehead point.

According to traditional Chinese acupuncture, we have a complex network of channels (meridians) within our body along which energy, or qi, travels. Acupuncture points are located on the surface of the body where the qi flows closest to the surface. There are 12 main meridians, with an estimated 365 acupuncture (or acupressure) points located along these meridians.

The Third Eye Point. In addition to the primary points, we also have some special points located outside of the primary pathways. One of these is the yintang point. The term "Yin" translates as seal, or central hall. So yintang can therefore be translated as "Hall of Seal" or "Central Mark."

The yintang point is located on your forehead midway between, and just above, your eyebrows. Many acupuncturists report that when treatments include this point, their patients feel a sense of clarity, get new insights into their lives, and are better able to make decisions that change the course and meaning of their lives. If you are using the services of an acupuncturist, you might want to explore this further with them.

Third Eye Acupressure Technique. Acupressure, a method of traditional Chinese medicine, is massage based upon the same concepts as acupuncture. You can stimulate your own third eye yintang point using controlled finger massage and pressure to adjust the flow of energy to your pineal gland/third eye point.

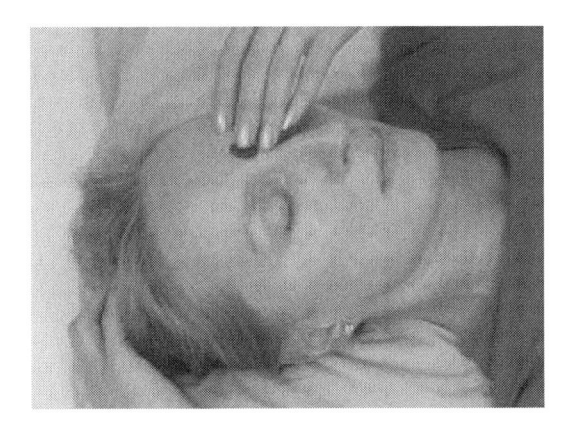

The yintang is located on the midline of your face, directly between and just above your eyebrows. Feel for a slight depression just beneath the skin.

By gently using the very end of your fingernail on this acupressure point you will quickly feel the effects of this mild stimulation.

Here are some special tips:

Breathe very deeply and slowly when performing acupressure on yourself or another person.

Focus your mind on your third eye acupressure point as you apply this stimulation.

Acupressure stimulation should feel strong, but should not create a sense of an uncomfortable level of pressure.

Be gentle with this point! I personally like to end this with gentle and extremely light "circle massage" on the entire area.

2. Brain Training

During my clinical EEG research beginning over 45 years ago I discovered some very specific brainwave frequencies that seem to be directly tied to ESP, lucid dreaming and other related psi (parapsychology) experiences.

ESP, for example, seems to be very consistently activated at about 3.7 cps Delta brainwaves, while those with frequent out-of-body experiences often demonstrate unusual activity at about 4.3 cps Theta brainwaves.

In my extensive research of a group of remarkable people in California's Silicon Valley I also noted that many highly successful and creative people could maintain conscious Theta and Delta brainwaves.

It is especially interesting to note that this unusual capability is learnable.

The use of brainwave training to initiate higher states of consciousness is more and more popular today. Also known as brainwave "entrainment," this method commonly uses audio stimulation only.

Third Eye Brainwave Stimulation. At certain brainwave frequencies such as deep Theta, a sense of your ego boundary often vanishes. Your consciousness is then less concerned with your "physical" state.

According to many ancient traditions, this corresponds to when your "third eye" begins to exhibit its special powers. If you have access to properly engineered Alpha-Theta brainwave audios, using them can increase your probability of opening your third eye.

Dr. Jill Ammon-Wexler

3. Chakra Stimulation

Chakra stimulation is an ancient art long used by yoga practitioners and meditators to heighten their awareness of their higher self.

According to the ancient chakra system, your nervous system network connects your sensory organs to the brain. Your chakras, in turn, are energy centers that function as pumps directing vital energy through this system.

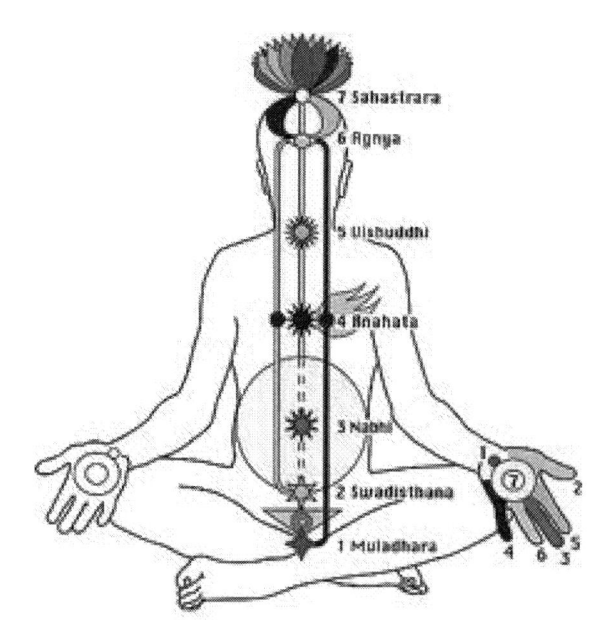

For example: Earth energy is drawn up through your lowest "root chakra" and channeled up to your "sacral chakra." The energy is then pumped up to your solar plexus chakra – then to your heart, throat, third eye (brow), and crown chakras.

The chakras are less dense than the physical body, and are said to interact with the physical body through two known physiological systems – the endocrine and nervous systems.

Many yoga and energy-based specialists say that when functioning well, our chakras are a conduit for the flow of energy throughout our entire body. It is therefore believed that tuning up your chakras can make an enormous difference to your sense of well-being and mental energy.

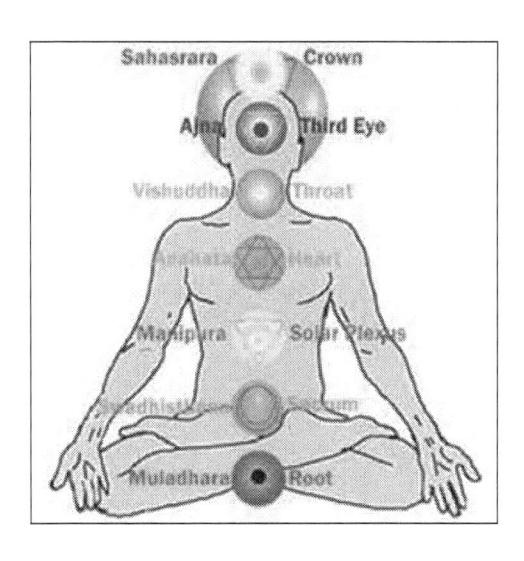

Two of these chakra energy centers specifically serve as the gateways to your higher self – the crown (sahasrara) chakra, and the third eye (ajna) chakra.

Activation of your important crown chakra is believed to be the key to fully experience yourself as "an integral part of the one omnipresent source of life" – the universal mind, or one consciousness.

The major chakra enhancement techniques include: meditation, certain forms of yoga, Kundalini yoga initiation, chakra visualization, sound meditation, breath work, acupressure and acupuncture, and brainwave entrainment.

Many of today's medical doctors are also using "energy medicine" techniques to balance their patient's chakra systems – respecting the ancient theory that the body is governed by a system of energy vortexes.

Chakra healing is also the source of many popular energy healing practices such as Yoga, Tai Chi, Acupuncture, Qi Gong and Reiki.

In one way or other, all of these practices look to the concept of chakras and the manipulation of energy. The breathing, stretching and meditative exercises used in Yoga, for example, often target the body's chakra system.

Tip: There's a recommended video and ebook to help you clear your chakras cited in the Reference section.

Your Third Eye Chakra. Each of your chakras controls a specific aspect of your life. Your third eye chakra controls your intuition and "knowing." This chakra is known in Sanskrit as *ajna*, which means "command," or "summoning."

It is also spoken of as the gate leading within to the inner realms of higher consciousness.

Our normal eyesight only lets us see the world through the filters of our limited beliefs, limiting our picture of the deeper reality behind what we can physically "see."

Since our third eye does not have such filters, we can presumably use it to view reality unlimited by our personal beliefs. With the opening of your third eye chakra, your intuitive "sixth sense" sharpens and you may find yourself more in tune with the universe.

Dr. Valerie V. Hunt, Professor of Physiological Science at the University of California at Los Angeles, has international acclaim in the fields of physiology, medicine and bioengineering.

Her groundbreaking research has led to the first truly scientific understanding of the relationship between energy field disturbances, disease and emotional imbalances. While conducting experiments with an electro-myograph – a medical device used to measure the electrical activity of muscles – Dr. Hunt was able to measure radiation emanating from the sites traditionally associated with the chakras in the bodies of her subjects.

Dr. Valerie Hunt

Activating a Chakra. Concentration on a chakra tends to activate it. After developing an instrument designed to detect minute electrical, magnetic and optical changes in the chakras, Dr. Hiroshi Motoyama conducted a scientific experiment on a normal person, and on a yoga practitioner with experience in chakra healing.

After monitoring the centers of his test subjects' stomachs and hearts, Motoyama found that the heart center of the yoga practitioner showed a considerable intensification of measurable activity during periods of concentration. Motoyama is the founder of the International Association for Religion and Parapsychology.

Third Eye Chakra Meditation Techniques. Many people spontaneously experience a third eye opening when they meditate or focus on healing themselves or others. If you want to consciously open your third eye during meditation, the following method will help.

Once settled into your meditation, visualize a vibrant indigo color or image behind your closed eyes. Gently focus your eyes on your third eye area. You may begin to feel a tingling sensation or slight pressure or vibration in that area.

This is an indication your third eye chakra is awakening, no matter how slight the sensation.

Often people begin to see shapes and colors of grey, white, purple and indigo before they actually get a clear vision of the third eye chakra.

The more you meditate and practice, the stronger colors you will see, until you finally experience at least a momentary third eye opening.

Sit quietly, clear your mind, and take a few slow deep breaths. Simply watch the images and colors behind your closed eyes. Relax, and breathe deeply and slowly. The colors may begin to take a shape, or seem to move out in front of you or toward the inside of your skull. Both sensations are fine.

What You're Experiencing. When you concentrate on a point inside or outside of your body, the chi energy of your body moves toward that point. Wherever you focus your mind, the energy follows. The chi will then collect and mass at that point, creating a silver light from the friction caused by the energy. Once you open your third eye you'll be able to see lights within and around your body.

The region of the third eye is a major collection point of chi stretching all the way from the perineum to the top of your head. If the chi channels below or above your third eye chakra are blocked or obstructed however, little energy will reach your third eye chakra.

The goal of this practice is to learn how to fix your mind on a single point with unwavering attention. Your chi from below will then rise up into the upper chakras and quiet your mind so that you can enter an advanced meditative state called samadhi. This technique is practiced in many schools of Taoism, Yoga, and Buddhism.

The opening of your third eye may also occur at unexpected moments, bringing with it a deep sense of bliss and a "connection" with all of life. Do not be disturbed if this wonderful sensation then fades – third eye opening is a process, and not necessarily a one-time event.

4. Chanting

Visualizing or focusing on your third eye while chanting is an especially powerful tool for directing your inner energies to activate your third eye.

Many systems claim that by focusing the inside of the brain at the midway point between the pineal gland and the pituitary body, a vibrating magnetic field can be created around the pineal gland.

One way to accomplish this is to chant certain sounds during your third eye visualization, or while meditating on an image of the third chakra.

Third Eye Chanting Method. Sit in a comfortable position and do some deep breathing to relax your body and mind. If you have access to brainwave training, you will benefit greatly by first listening to a professionally engineered Alpha or an Alpha/Theta brainwave training.

Step 1. Sit in a comfortable posture with your back straight and leaning slightly forward from the back of your chair.

Step 2. Take a few deep breaths in through your nose all the way down to your lower abdomen, then exhale it out through your mouth and let it remove all of your tension.

Step 3. Once settled in, begin to gently focus your eyes on the point just above and in the middle of your eyebrows. You do NOT have to actually focus your physical eyes on this point – you can also simply visualize looking at that point. Relax your eyes – do not overly strain them.

Step 4. Imagine an indigo or purple color in front of your third eye. Watch it, and sense its pulsating energy.

Step 5. Chant a C tone you can feel tingling in your head, throat, and especially on your forehead. I personally find that the Om chant works very well for this, and is the best sound for third eye activation.

Women: If you have a high voice, allow your voice to drop down lower in your throat until you can feel the vibration as you chant.

Step 6. Continue to chant and focus on the resulting vibration in your head.

Do not force a picture to appear, and simply observe any that do appear without analysis.

Note: If you're not familiar with the Om or Aum sound, here's a free "Om audio" online that you can listen to or download:"

http://mp3.tamilwire.com/chanting-om-vinayagar-murugan.html

5. Hypnosis & Visualization

Hypnosis is highly recommended by some alternative therapists as an excellent method of opening your third eye.

Although it's not impossible to achieve this end result, no research evidence has yet surfaced. However guided visualization and hypnosis can be excellent for preparing yourself for such an opening experience.

The benefit is the proven ability of these tools to induce the "Relaxation Response." Research suggests that hypnotic subjects are fully awake and focusing attention, and yet are deeply relaxed.

6. Progressive Relaxation Method

One of the best ways to relax in preparation for third eye opening is the "Progressive Relaxation" method developed by physician Edmund Jacobson in the 1920s.

This method is even today used by elite athletes around the world. Progressive muscle relaxation (PMR) involves systematically and alternately tensing and relaxing the muscles over your entire body.

You can make a tape of the following progressive relaxation method. Be sure to read slowly and in a relaxed voice. Pause briefly after each command.

Relax on the bed on your back and gently close your eyes.

Focus on your feet. Consciously relax them and let them sink down into the bed. Now progress to your ankles.

Focus on your knees and sense their weight or any tension. Consciously relax your knees and feel them sink deeper into the bed.

Focus on your upper legs and thighs. Feel any tension, then consciously relax them and let them sink into the bed.

Focus on your abdomen and chest. Notice your breathing, and will it to slow and relax. Deepen your breathing a bit and let your abdomen and chest sink down into the bed.

Focus on your buttocks. Sense any tension or tightness. Consciously relax them and let them sink down into the bed.

Now focus on your hands. Consciously relax any tension in your hands and feel them sink into the bed.

Become aware of your upper arms. Consciously relax them until they sink into the bed.

Sense your shoulders and relax any tension in them until they sink down into the bed.

Become aware of your neck. Consciously relax any tight muscles until your head sinks deeper into the bed.

Focus on your mouth and jaw. Consciously relax them and unclench your jaw and face muscles.

Sense if there is any tension in your eyes or you are forcing your eyelids closed. Relax your eyes and eyelids.

Focus on your face and cheeks and consciously relax them.

Now mentally scan your entire body. If you find tension, consciously relax that part of your body. Then just release yourself.

Note: A 7-minute guided downloadable visualization that will effortlessly guide you through Progressive Relaxation is available as part of the complete "Third Eye Audio Collection" at=>

http://www.QuantumLeapAudios.com

7. Third Eye Mudra

You can use an ancient East Indian yoga mudra method to open your third eye chakra. Mudras are special hand positions believed by yogis to have the power to direct more energy to specific chakras.

3rd Eye Mudra

To enhance the effect for third eye activation, simultaneously chant the Aum or Om sound as you hold the mudra position.

Using the Third Eye Mudra. Here's how to use a traditional yogic third eye mudra for pineal gland/third eye activation:

Third Eye Mudra

Position your hands in front of the lower part of your breast.

Your middle fingers should remain straight and touch at the tops while pointing forward.

Your other fingers are bent and touch at the upper portions of the fingers.

Your thumbs should point toward you and touch at their tops.

Close your physical eyes and mentally focus your inner vision on the position of your third eye chakra on your forehead – in between and just above the eyebrows.

Do not strain your physical eyes.

Chant Om or Aum while remaining relaxed and contemplative.

8. Reflexology

Here is a great tip that may surprise you – you can apply reflexology to certain points on your big toes to stimulate the vitality of your pineal gland.

These points are actually located on proven acupuncture meridians. Use your index finger to press in and down on the little ledge on the medial side of your big toes, just above the bump and even with the base of the nail.

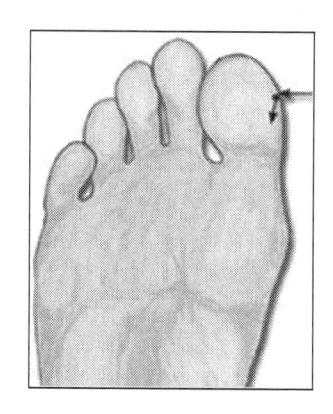

9. Kundalini Energy

A fully achieved Yogi master can awakened your Kundalini by a direct transfer of their energy to you. This powerful experience, known as Shaktipat, activates your dormant Kundalini energy.

"Shakti" means power or energy in Sanskrit, and "pat" means transfer. Thus Shaktipat is a transfer of energy that opens the flow of energy through all of the chakras, including your third eye chakra.

Shaktipat Initiation. The transmission of energy to an aspirant is accomplished by the touch, gaze, sound or thought of a Yogi master. The process of Shaktipat can be performed only by advanced yogis who have gained complete control over their life force – referred to as prana in Sanskrit.

Some people have fears about activating their Kundalini, but it is absolutely safe to practice Kundalini Maha Yoga under the guidance of a fully realized spiritual teacher.

Note: I personally experienced a Kundalini Yoga Shaktipat initiation from Shri Anandi Ma, the spiritual heir of Shri Dhyanyogi Madhusudandas, an East Indian saint and renowned Master of Kundalini Maha Yoga born in Bihar, India.

Shri Anandi Ma gazed at me while touching my forehead with a peacock feather. The force of the touch of that feather unexpectedly catapulted me backward toward the floor, and instantly opened an entirely new state of reality that has continued to flourish to this day.

Shri Anandi Ma can be contacted at the Antioch, California Dhyanyogi Center. She also travels regularly throughout the USA, India and Europe offering meditation programs and Shaktipat Initiation to sincere seekers.

Shri Anandi Ma

In addition she offers periodic workshops and retreats during which she personally instructs students in ancient yogic practices and techniques only passed down from teacher to student.

The center's website is: http://dyc.org/

10. Tapping

Although many "tapping experts" recommend tapping the third eye position as part of a tapping series, only one I'm aware of recommends specifically tapping just the third eye chakra – Carol Tuttle.

Tapping the Third Eye. According to tapping expert Carol Tuttle, the best time to tap your third eye chakra is when you are already feeling "joy, hope, happiness, excitement, peace or any other positive feeling" and you want to "anchor those positive energies."

"This chakra assists you with insight, intuitions, seeing the bigger picture, connecting with your soul-knowing, all the energies that help you feel good. When you want to anchor in a positive emotion," Tuttle says, "tap on this point with your fingertips for about 20-30 seconds."

At the same time Tuttle recommends you say the following out loud or to yourself: "I am grateful I am feeling better and better more and more of the time."

Tuttle's method is very likely taking advantage of the acupressure sensitivity of your third eye chakra.

11. Alternate Nostril Breathing

Indian yoga pranayama breathing dates back thousands of years. Your nose is directly linked to your brain and nervous system.

The evidence is that breathing only through your left nostril accesses the right "feeling" hemisphere of your brain, and breathing only through your right nostril accesses the left "thinking" hemisphere of your brain.

Consciously alternating your breath between your nostrils can therefore allow you to activate and access your whole brain.

Alternate nostril breathing is a yoga breathing technique that calms the mind and seems to directly energize the third eye chakra. You can perform it as follows:

Rest the base of the palm of your right hand on your chin, and your three middle fingers on your forehead. If necessary rest your elbow on a table or desk.

Gently press your left nostril closed with your little finger, and breathe in through your right nostril.

Now close your right nostril with your thumb, and slowly breathe out through your left nostril.

Next, breathe in through your left nostril, while your thumb holds the right nostril closed.

Finally, breathe out through your right nostril, while holding your left nostril closed with your little finger.

Repeat this process until your mind is clear of thoughts and feels relaxed.

Once your mind is quiet and relaxed, rest your hands on your lap or on a table and begin slow deep breathing through your nose.

Eventually you will slip into a very deep meditative state.

If you have enough residual energy from this breathing exercise, your third eye or crown chakra will awaken, you will see brilliant flashes of light inside your brain, and you will experience a sensation of bliss.

Note: Do not hold your breath if you have high blood pressure. Most people find that practicing this on an empty stomach works best.

12. Third Eye Breathing

Here's another breathing exercise to specifically open your third eye chakra using alternating nostril breathing.

Start by closing your right nostril with one finger. While keeping your right nostril closed, begin to take a long deep breath through the left nostril.

Visualize the stream of breath making its way to the center of your forehead where your third eye chakra is located.

Now close your left nostril and slowly exhale through your right nostril.

Visualize that same stream of air traveling back from your forehead and out your nostril.

Keeping your left nostril closed, inhale once again out your right nostril. Close that nostril, and exhale out of the left. Repeat the visualization of the stream of air traveling back into the third eye chakra in your forehead.

Note: This is a time-tested yoga technique, but it's not good to overdo it. Do not exceed ten rounds of this style of alternate breathing, and you may wish to avoid it completely if you have asthma or other breathing problems. If you have any doubt, always check first with your personal health practitioner.

13. Yantra Meditation

The energy of your chakras vibrates in an orderly sequence of seven distinct frequencies, just like the notes of the musical scale. The colors of the spectrum also represent a series of seven vibrations in a logical and orderly sequence.

Music played in a certain key vibrates a particular chakra. You may not be consciously aware of it, but you tend to feel certain emotions when you hear

PINEAL GLAND & YOUR THIRD EYE

music in each key. Our relationship with a certain color also says something about our relationship with the aspect of our consciousness (or chakra) represented by that particular color.

The third eye ajna chakra corresponds to the musical note C, and to the colors indigo and violet. It therefore follows that focusing on these colors, or listening to or chanting in the key of C, will help activate your third eye chakra.

In the yogic tradition, mantras, the Sanskrit syllables inscribed on yantras, are essentially "thought forms" representing divinities or cosmic powers, which exert their influence by means of sound-vibrations.

Yantra meditation is a long-standing yogic method of developing your connection to a specific chakra and its properties.

Try focusing on a third eye Om yantra with soft eyes during a meditation or contemplation session. You can even further the strength of your meditation by chanting "Om" as you do so.

Note: Do a search on the web for a "yantra third eye image" and download a suitable colored image for your personal use.

14. Balasana Yoga Pose

Gently rocking your forehead while doing the Yoga balasana (child's pose) to massage the brow center can open the energy flow to your third eye chakra.

Kneel on the floor or on a yoga or exercise mat. Touch your big toes together and sit on your heels, then separate your knees about as wide as your hips.

Exhale and lower your torso down between your thighs. Broaden your sacrum across the back of your pelvis and narrow your hip points so that they rest down onto your inner thighs.

Lengthen your tailbone away from the back of the pelvis while you lift the base of your skull away from the back of your neck.

Place your hands on the floor alongside your torso with palms up, then release your shoulders toward the floor.

Allow the weight of your shoulders to pull your shoulder blades open across your back.

Finally, hold this position from 30 seconds to a few minutes. Rock your forehead gently on the floor or mat.

To come up, first lengthen your torso, then inhale and lift slowly from your tailbone.

15. Third Eye Visualization

Visualization is always a very powerful way to activate your pineal gland and encourage your third eye to open. This method may seem much more comfortable to you if you are not a meditator, or do not practice yoga.

To prepare for third eye visualization, begin by settling into a comfortable position, either sitting up or lying down. If you fall asleep easily when lying down, sit upright instead.

Take steps to relax your body.

Once your whole body feels relaxed, shift your focus to your breathing. Visualize feeling lighter and lighter with each inhale, and letting go of any tension or worry with each exhale.

To begin your third eye visualization, shift your attention to the place between your eyes on your forehead.

Imagine your head surrounded by a glowing indigo or violet light.

Visualize your pineal gland as a glowing area directly in the center of your head.

Envision a bright fluorescent light streaming out of your pineal gland.

Picture the light becoming brighter and brighter until you can feel it tingling and heating your forehead, and especially the area above and between your eyebrows.

When you feel ready to finish your third eye meditation, slowly move or wiggle your fingers and toes, then open your eyes and take a few deep breaths.

Note: If your third eye area ever feels uncomfortably overheated, stop your exercise, breath in some lavender or peppermint oil, and place a cool wet wash cloth over your forehead.

16. Essential Oils

The third eye chakra governs your brain, your entire neurological system, your eyes, ears, nose, and your pituitary and pineal glands.

Physical dysfunctions of this chakra are believed to be the possible cause of brain tumors, strokes, blindness, deafness, seizures, panic, depression and confusion.

Oils For the Third Eye. Essential oils believed to support the third eye are said to carry a high energetic frequency. The most popular of these oils include: frankincense, neroli, elemi, rose, jasmine, melissa, lavender and sandalwood. A good method of use is to simply apply a bit of your preferred oil to a handkerchief or your collar.

Headaches and migraines can be related to a stressed and tense third eye chakra. Common essential oils for headaches include: lavender, tea tree, eucalyptus, jasmine, peppermint, hyssop, melissa, chamomile, marjoram and rosemary. Again, an application to a handkerchief or collar is the preferred method of use.

Dr. Jill Ammon-Wexler

FOUR: ARE YOU PSYCHIC?

Doctor Chris Roe places a pair of enormous fluffy earphones over the head of a blonde 20-year-old woman. He then carefully slices a ping-pong ball in half and tapes each piece over her eyes, switches on a red light that bathes the woman in an eerie glow, and leaves the room.

After a few moments, a low hum fills the laboratory, and the woman begins to smile as images of distant locations begin to flow through her mind. She says she can sense a group of trees and a babbling brook full of boulders. Standing on one boulder is her friend Jack waving at her and smiling. She begins to describe the location to Doctor Roe.

Half a mile away, her friend Jack is, indeed, standing on a boulder in a stream. Somehow, the woman has been able to see Jack in her mind's eye, even though common sense says this is impossible.

Doctor Roe, a parapsychologist based at the University of Northampton, is investigating if it's possible to project your mind to a distant location to observe what's happening there. His early findings suggest that up to 85% of us are naturally clairvoyant and possess remote viewing abilities. And he believes that with only minimum training, we can ALL develop these psychic skills.

"Our results are significant," Roe says. "Psychic skills are something that should be taken seriously."

An increasing number of scientists agree with him. Professor Brian Josephson, a Nobel Prize physicist at Cambridge University, says: "The experiments have been designed to rule out luck and chance. I consider the evidence pretty clear-cut."

In 1995, the US Congress asked two independent scientists to assess whether the millions the government had spent on psychic research had produced anything of value.

The conclusions proved somewhat unexpected. Professor Jessica Utts, a statistician at the University of California, discovered that remote viewers were correct 34 per cent of the time – a figure far beyond what chance guessing would produce.

Utts concluded: "Using the standards applied to any area of science, you have to conclude that certain psychic phenomena, such as remote viewing, have been well established. The results are not due to chance or flaws in the experiments."

Developing your "conscious self" psychic abilities begins with refining and developing your awareness of who YOU are. The remainder of this book focuses on this from a very practical science and psychology focus.

Regardless of your metaphysical or religious convictions, this simply comes down to how your individual "persona" chooses to deal with your day-to-day reality.

Dr. Jill Ammon-Wexler

FIVE: AWARENESS

Until recently science believed we were separate from the rest of life; but modern Field Theory and Quantum Physics now suggest a totally different view of what exists "in here" and "out there."

One of the most interesting concepts of modern Field Theory is that ALL of life exists as a single unified conscious field – an interwoven consciousness in which each part affects the whole at every moment. Understood in these terms, your "higher self" is already connected to this conscious universal source of life.

Here's the science behind this: As scientists explore smaller and smaller portions of what was once thought to be the smallest (the atom), they finally end up exploring something far different yet.

he term "zero-point field" was created to refer to this unknown invisible field that seems to exist at the very core of sub-atomic reality.

Dr. Jill Ammon-Wexler

Science has now confirmed that, at the most extremely small immeasurable level of reality, there is still some unknown force present. This is true even at the temperature of absolute zero, when all known forms of energy seem to vanish.

But reality at this level isn't exactly "energy," nor is it a field of empty space. It is described by physicists as a field of information.

Physicist, futurist and author Ervin Laszlo

Physicist Ervin Laszlo calls this field the "A-field" – perhaps referring to the ancient Vedic concept of the "Akashic record," a nonphysical repository of all knowledge in the universe, including all human experience.

Laszlo says, "The ancients knew that space is not empty, it is the origin and memory of all things that exist and have ever existed.

This insight is now being rediscovered at the cutting edge of the sciences [and is emerging] as a main pillar of the scientific world's picture of the twenty-first century. This will profoundly change our concept of ourselves and of the world."

Personal Empowerment

Any personal empowerment goal has to begin with where you are today. So the logical place for you to start is by asking yourself how clear and aware you are right now? In short – what's the current level of your self-awareness?

We all automatically assume that we ARE self aware. But there are actually different levels of self-awareness? Have you ever been involved in a serious automobile accident? If so, you probably experienced everything (including your thoughts) moving in slow motion. You were super-aware of each tiny detail of your situation, and of your ongoing thought process.

What was happening? You stepped into hyper-awareness of the timeless and spaceless universal field of consciousness that modern Field Theory is referring to.

Such a state of extremely heightened self-awareness only lasts a few milliseconds; but during that time your senses are ultra acute, your thoughts very ordered, and hopefully your actions are very appropriate.

There are other levels of hyper-awareness that are much more inviting that those you might experience when facing possible death. You can learn to enter into these types of heightened states with some practice using either meditation or engineered brainwave training.

There are also many levels of self-awareness below hyper-awareness. You have likely experienced exhaustion in your lifetime – the physical and mental wipe out that leaves you listless and collapsed on the couch. How self-aware were you then?

Build Your Self-Awareness

Self-awareness is a core aspect of success in any aspect of life. Where you focus your attention, emotions, reactions, personality and behavior absolutely determines what you can achieve.

Refined self-awareness allows you to make better decisions to shape your future. It also gives you a sense of having a purpose and direction, and makes you more effective in your work, business, relationships, and every aspect of your life. It is also an important step to opening your third eye and experiencing higher states of consciousness.

Experiencing Hyper-Awareness

Many years ago I had the pleasure of spending Sunday afternoons with a small group of like-minded people visiting philosopher Alan Watts on his houseboat in California's colorful Sausalito Bay.

Just in case Alan's name is not familiar to you, he was a British writer and speaker best known as a popularizer of Eastern philosophy.

Watts wrote over 25 books and articles, including "The Way of Zen" – a best-selling book on Buddhism. He also explored human consciousness in another popular book, "The Joyous Cosmology."

We spent those Sunday afternoons enjoying the crisp ocean air, red wine and San Francisco sourdough bread as Alan reflected on the nature of life. He shared the insightful wisdom of the Asian philosophies, and often reminded us of one simple key: "If you want to achieve enlightened consciousness, you only need to do one thing – BE HERE NOW!"

Alan Watt's houseboat "The Vallejo"

The following exercise can help you tap into hyper-awareness on an actual brain level – the "Circle Breath" exercise Watts led us into during many of those Sunday afternoons.

Settle into a comfortable position on a chair, or sit on a cushion on the floor, and let your mind begin to lightly and naturally follow your breath.

At first just notice how you draw air in and out totally naturally. Become comfortably aware of your breath as an effortless "steady flow."

Once comfortable, begin to create a rhythm by breathing in through your nose to a count of 1 - 2 - 3.

When you reach 3, pause, and gently hold your breath for a count of 1 - 2 - 3.

Once you reach 3, slowly and gently release your breath in a steady stream to a count of 1 - 2 - 3 - 4 - 5.

Repeat the pattern. At first practice this method for 2 to 3 minutes. As you become better attuned to breath control, extend your time.

When you feel ready, just return your attention to your normal breathing pattern.

Most of us never think of controlling our breath, but this exercise can open the door to higher states of awareness and consciousness.

Eventually your breathing will become a continuous circle. What comes with such an experience of "circle breath" is an ecstatic experience of momentarily stepping into the timeless universal consciousness.

Note: This breathing method may obviously not feel natural at first. Just relax, follow your "in" breath, pause lightly, and then release your "out" breath.

Your breath control should come from your abdomen, not your chest. Let your abdominal muscles pull your breath in deeply and quietly without strain, and then use your abdominal muscles to push the air back out very gently.

While doing this exercise avoid being tense in your chest, stomach and face. If your body gets tense, just relax and just continue to focus on your breath.

SIX: MOTIVATION & HIGHER STATES

Back in the 1940s an American psychologist – Dr. Abraham Maslow – came up with a brilliant explanation of what pushes us to reach toward higher states of awareness and consciousness. His explanation is so clear that you'll immediately "get it."

Maslow stacked our basic human "needs" in the shape of a pyramid. He then explained that although we are naturally motivated to climb the pyramid, we have to climb it one step at a time.

Maslow explained that until you have satisfied the "needs" at a lower level of the pyramid, you aren't motivated to step up onto the next higher level.

So if you are focused on a "physiological survival level" need for food or drink, you won't be motivated to strive toward the top level of higher states (self actualization) that could include third eye activation.

This obviously makes sense. Let's review how this might work in your brain.

Dr. Jill Ammon-Wexler

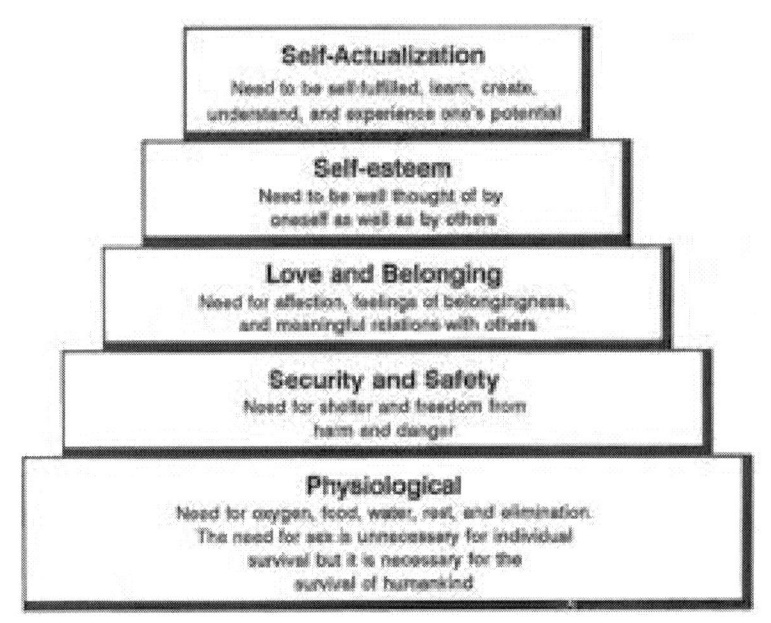

Maslow's Hierarchy of Needs

- **Self-Actualization**: Need to be self-fulfilled, learn, create, understand, and experience one's potential
- **Self-esteem**: Need to be well thought of by oneself as well as by others
- **Love and Belonging**: Need for affection, feelings of belongingness, and meaningful relations with others
- **Security and Safety**: Need for shelter and freedom from harm and danger
- **Physiological**: Need for oxygen, food, water, rest, and elimination. The need for sex is unnecessary for individual survival but it is necessary for the survival of humankind

Motivation and the Brain

Your personal mental state of consciousness and self-awareness reflect your ability to enter into certain brain-based mental states. Let's take a closer look at how Maslow's levels look in terms of your brain:

The Survival Level. "Physiological survival" level challenges activate your lower brain stem. The brain stem is NOT a conscious "thinking" center.

Your brain stem is in charge of monitoring incoming sensory information, and its job is to then determine if what's happening is important enough to send up to your higher brain centers. It is often referred to as your "reptilian brain."

If you're lost in the desert and need water, your brain stem will scan every possible external clue trying to direct you to water. This obviously does NOT activate the portions of your brain used to experience higher states of consciousness.

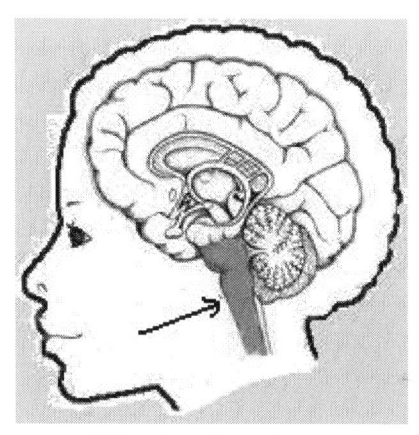

The brain stem

The Emotional Level. As you move up on Maslow's pyramid you next focus in a higher portion of your brain – the limbic center..

The limbic center is your brain's emotional center, and is primarily concerned with "security and safety" issues. It dominates the large center potion of your brain

When you're caught up in an intense emotional response, this is where your brain is focused. In such a situation the limbic center overrides your cortex – the part of your brain responsible for rational and logical thinking.

The limbic center is NOT the part of your brain that connects you with your higher self, although it IS active in higher states experiences.

The Logical Level. As you begin your search for greater self mastery, you will focus more and more in the more rational, logical portion of your brain known as the cerebral cortex. Your cortex is a thin sheet of neural tissue that's wrapped around the outside of the brain and is often called your "thinking cap."

The cortex plays a key role in your memory, attention, awareness, thought, and both ordinary and higher states of consciousness. The cerebral cortex is also a gateway to your higher consciousness, but there's something special that has to occur for you to get beyond its natural emphasis on logical analysis.

The Higher States Level. Having direct access to your higher self (and opening your third eye) is a unique experience that feels like a light bulb suddenly turning on in the brain – or may seem like a gentle "glow" and wonderful feeling of well-being.

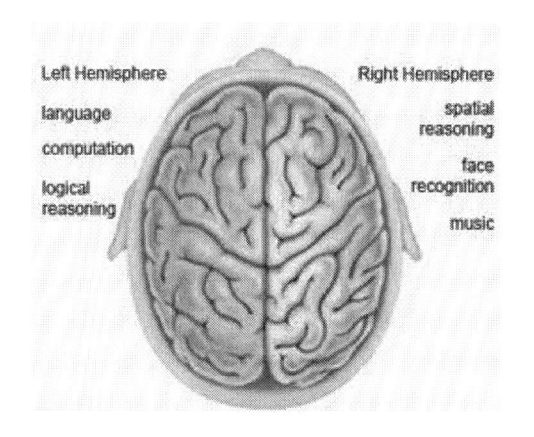

The two hemispheres of your cortex

Notice in the above picture how your brain is split in two halves right down the middle. A higher states experience occurs when the two sides of your cortex are balanced and resonating at the same brainwave frequency.

This creates a glowing feeling of well-being, great peacefulness, third eye activation, higher states of consciousness and awareness, natural psychic abilities, increased intuitive understanding and knowing, unusually clear senses, and feeling as though you somehow extend beyond your physical body.

Dr. Jill Ammon-Wexler

SEVEN: SELF-AWARENESS

Self-awareness is refined by beginning to consciously focus on your own moment-to-moment thoughts and behavior.

As you increase your awareness of your own thoughts, emotions and behavior you will automatically move toward more exciting levels of higher consciousness.

As you become more and more self aware, you'll begin to notice aspects of your personality and behavior you didn't see before. If you feel frustrated, for example, you'll begin to more clearly understand exactly what created your feeling of frustration and why.

You'll also notice you can consciously choose how to interpret something. In your heightened awareness you'll instinctively make better choices long before a knee-jerk emotional reaction erupts.

Capturing "Now"

Remember Alan Watt's recommendation to "BE HERE NOW?" Is it challenging to totally focus in the present moment? Yes it is! Our normal everyday "monkey mind" prefers to roam around from the past to the future.

Being totally focused and present NOW is the goal of most meditation programs, serious yoga practices, and any effort to open your third eye and develop your natural intuitive and psychic abilities.

Committing to become aware of your thoughts and behavior will move you toward being here now, as Watts recommended. Changing your thoughts and behavior becomes far easier when you develop your self-awareness, as you can then more easily catch and control undesired behavior and thought patterns before they gather momentum.

Building Your Personal Power

The purpose of increasing your self-awareness is to better understand yourself, then use that knowledge to make ongoing life improvements. But before you can make positive changes, you have to know what you have to work with.

If you really DO have a desire to attain higher levels of consciousness, you'll want to put aside some time to frequently reflect on your thoughts and actions. This will open you to a deeper understanding of your dreams, values, beliefs and assumptions.

Emotional Awareness. An important aspect of self-awareness is emotional awareness. This involves the ability to recognize the emotions you experience, understand the feelings associated with them, and be aware of what you think and do as a result of your emotions.

Emotions are very powerful indicators of your level of self-awareness. They rise up out of an older portion of your brain (the limbic center), and are accompanied by a resulting biochemical response that affects your entire physical body.

There is nothing inherently wrong with emotions – they are a natural component of our human expression and experience. Refine your ability to recognize and understand them, and you will develop the ability to use your emotions as a tool to develop higher states of consciousness.

Awareness Exercise 1. The goal of the following self-awareness exercise is to learn to avoid knee-jerk emotional outbreaks to events and emotions, and refine your ability to CHOOSE your emotional response to any situation. Analyze what's happening with your emotions, and your self-awareness will skyrocket.

Begin to carry a little notebook around with you. As soon as possible after you experience an intense emotion ... then spend a few moments noting what happened.

Write down the emotion you experienced, and what you felt at the time was the "cause" of your emotion. If another driver cut you off and you get angry, note something like "other driver."

If you felt stressed because of a deadline at work, note "deadline." Then note what happened just before that event, and how you were feeling at the time.

Finally, try to reframe your emotion by thinking of it as your RESPONSE to the other driver, or your RESPONSE to the stress at work.

You may experience a conflict in your mind about who or what was "responsible" for your emotional reaction. Use higher self-awareness to remind yourself that it was your own personal RESPONSE to what happened that created any undesirable emotion.

This process will immediately raise your self-awareness and ability to remind yourself that you have a choice. You can execute a knee-jerk emotional reaction to what happens, OR you can CHOOSE to respond in a more self-aware manner. This moves you UP on Maslow's pyramid.

Awareness Exercise 2. Practice the following exercise to expand your level of awareness. Although this may seem "mundane," it will create some important changes in your brain that will move you toward higher levels of awareness and consciousness.

Pick an everyday activity for this exercise, and repeat it at least once a day this week. Select something you normally do on "automatic" without thinking about it – perhaps like making your bed, eating lunch, showering, or washing dishes.

Your goal is to go into hyper-awareness while doing this activity – to stop time, and operate in "super-conscious, higher awareness slow motion."

The following example is for washing a few dishes left from lunch. [Translate it to your selected activity.]

Walk to the sink and "position yourself" to wash dishes. Notice the sensation of your feet on the floor, and bend your knees to take the pressure off your lower back. Roll up your sleeves one at a time.

Turn the hot water faucet on. Notice the feel of the metal against your hand. Look at the faucet and notice the seal of the manufacturer, the arch of the spout, and how the water comes out of the spout.

Adjust the water to the correct temperature and notice how the hot water feels on your hands. How would you describe the sensation? Look at your hands in the water. How is the water flowing? Are there bubbles or splashes?

Briefly look out the window above the sink. How does the view impact your emotions? How many different colors can you see? How many shapes?

Pick up the sponge in one hand and the bottle of dish soap in the other hand. What is the weight of each? Notice how your hands automatically balance the difference in weight between the two.

Wet the sponge, then squirt a bit of dish soap on it. What color is the soap? What color is the sponge? What is the look of the soap on the sponge? How would you describe its consistency? Is there a scent? What does it remind you of?

Place the bottle of soap back on the counter-top and lift the first plate. What is the feeling of the plate in your hand? Notice the design. Are there any chips or scratches?

Use the sponge to apply soapy water to the surface of the plate. How does the soapy water feel on your hands? What changes occur in the surface of the plate?

You get the picture! Bring as much consciousness and awareness to your actions as possible. Take your time and BE HERE NOW.

Dr. Jill Ammon-Wexler

EIGHT: HIGHER INTELLIGENCE

Is there some inside secret to turning on your higher mental states and activating your third eye? YES, and it's most easily understood by learning a bit more about how your brain does what it does.

With few exceptions, our parents and educational systems focused on developing our "rational, logical" minds – often at the expense of our intuitive, natural connection to our higher selves.

How does this impact your ability to explore your higher self? To better understand this, let's first explore the nature of what we call "intelligence" and the many forms it can take

What IS Intelligence?

You really have several different layers of what is commonly called "intelligence." Let's take a brief look at them.

Your IQ Intelligence. I'm certain you're familiar with the most common description of your intelligence IQ.

The term IQ stands for "Intelligence Quotient," and is a score that is assigned to you based on your performance on a standardized intelligence test developed many years ago.

For years a person's IQ score was assumed to be a true measure of their level of intelligence. If you scored 100, you were of "average" intelligence, 110-119 indicated you had "superior" intelligence, 120 to 139 equaled "very superior" intelligence, and 140 and over made you a genius.

However, the test that measures IQ was only designed to measure a certain type of intelligence. Your IQ score is primarily a measure of your linear, straight-line logical way of thinking. It is 1+1=2. This way of thinking primarily uses the information you stored in your brain from formal learning experiences. Remember learning your "times tables?"

Your EQ Intelligence. Your EQ is your "Emotional Intelligence," and is based on your life experience practical intelligence. EQ is not straight line, logical thinking like IQ thinking. EQ thinking asks your brain to search for new meanings to your life experiences.

Many companies today give EQ tests to potential new executives. The evidence is that EQ predicts a person's communication skills, thinking flexibility, and leadership potential far better than their IQ.

Your HQ Intelligence. Here's one you might not have heard of before – your HQ, or "Higher Intelligence." Your higher intelligence is a very special part of your mental processes.

HQ is the source of the unusual synchronized wave of energy that ripples over your cortex when you connect to your higher self, get a brilliant idea, or pop open your third eye.

During an HQ experience you may feel your brain vibrating, or even experience a flash of light in your head.

HQ is your direct connection into the "unified higher mind" that Carl Jung and Albert Einstein referred to, and to the field of consciousness of Field Theory.

Your HQ produces religious ecstasy, enlightenment, brilliant insights, third eye opening, and deep intuitive understanding of the nature of life and your life purpose.

Increasing Your HQ

You might wonder why HQ experiences are so infrequent, and even impossible, for some people.

There is an obvious social reason for this, since our societies do not necessarily reward HQ thinking.

Our educational systems are primarily designed to increase IQ-related thinking, and our teachers encourage us to stop daydreaming and "pay attention."

And why are HQ-related experiences seemingly more frequent for women? This too is a socially-created phenomenon. It's more likely for girls to be encouraged to pursue activities involving imagination and fantasies, while boys are often directed toward non-fantasy activities such as sports.

The real reason HQ experiences are so rare has to do with the lack of a very specific brain-based condition. Read on.

NINE. THE SPEED OF THOUGHT

Did you realize that your brain produces enough electricity (about 10 watts) to light up the inside of your refrigerator? It's actually an electro-chemical marvel.

Each of your thoughts can be viewed on an EEG screen as they pass through your brain creating electrical currents called "brainwaves." Brainwaves result from the tiny electro-chemical messages that move your thoughts along from one neuron (brain cell) to another along a pathway called a neural network.

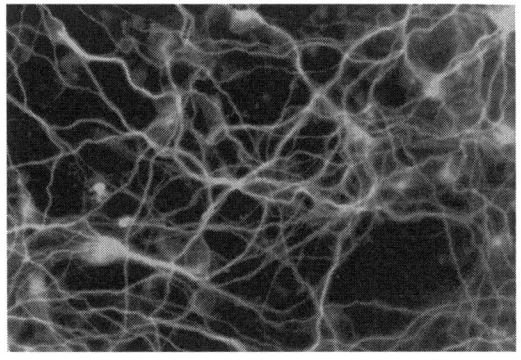

A neural network

Depending on what mental state you are in, your brainwaves may be very fast (stress) or very slow (deep sleep.) Scientists group your brainwaves according to their "frequency," which is a measure of the number of "on-off" cycles during a given period of time (a second).

Delta Brainwaves

Your slowest brainwaves are the Delta brainwaves normally associated with deep dreamless sleep. Delta brainwaves have a frequency range of about .05 cps (cycles-per-second) to 3.9 cps.

It might be normal to assume that these slow "deep sleep" brainwaves have very little to do with exploring your higher self and higher states of consciousness. Actually, just the opposite is true.

Delta brainwaves are very well developed in psychics, artists and writers, mystics, creative scientists, and people capable of unusual intuition and psi (ESP) experiences. During my EEG brainwave

research I discovered that ESP phenomena often occur in connection with conscious 3.7 cps (high Delta) brainwave activity.

Theta Brainwaves

The next faster brainwaves are the Theta brainwaves associated with both light and dreaming sleep. Theta brainwaves have a frequency range of 4.0 to 7.9 cps. Theta may also be considered to be the "voice" of your subconscious mind.

Theta is also a doorway to expanded states of consciousness and awareness. The challenge is that unless you have had considerable meditation training, your Theta brainwaves simply automatically drop you into a sleeping state, but this can be overcome with focused brain training programs.

Alpha Brainwaves

Alpha brainwaves operate in a frequency of 8.0 to 11.9 cps. Alpha is the brainwave frequency of relaxation and creativity.

The lower range of Alpha is actually the doorway or gate between your conscious and subconscious mind. Learning to open this gate gives you conscious access to your storehouse of subconscious materials.

Beta Brainwaves

Your Beta brainwaves operate in a frequency of 12.0 to about 23 cps. Beta brainwaves are the voice of your conscious mind, and are activated anytime you think or speak, even silently to yourself.

Gamma Brainwaves

Your Gamma brainwaves operate in a frequency of 24 cps and higher. Beta and Gamma brainwaves are often associated with stress or a "racing mind." The exception to this is the 40 cps range experienced by long experienced meditators, or those in a state of bliss.

Brainwaves & Higher States

So ... what do your brainwaves look like when you have an active connection with your higher self or open your third eye? This is a greatly misunderstood subject.

In spite of claims made by some sources of "brain entrainment" CDs – a single brainwave like Alpha is NOT responsible for creating a higher mental state experience. Actually, higher states experiences result from a simultaneous combination of brainwaves ranging from Delta to Beta, and even touching into the Gamma level for some people.

The most obvious question you may now have is: "How can I achieve this brainwave state?" One way to achieve what I call the "Quantum Mind brainwave state" can be approached through years of disciplined meditation.

Sone serious seekers retreat to caves in the Himalayas or monasteries and commit their lives to living as much as possible in a state of meditation. If this is not your path, what choices do you have?

Hypnosis and guided meditation are also a great way to relax and drop down into lower Alpha brainwaves. That is always beneficial, but will not train your brain to reach higher states or open your third eye.

Engineered brainwave audios are a serious improvement, especially if used in a way to actually train your brain to create the desired states on its own.

The best training audios contain an engineered combination of selected frequencies (ie, high Alpha down through low Theta and high Delta), and ramp you up and down into an optimal and safe brainwave entrainment experience.

Dr. Jill Ammon-Wexler

TEN. PINEAL GLAND HEALTH

It is important to be aware of how fluorides impact your body. The calcium fluoride found naturally in underground water supplies is relatively benign.

On the other hand, the synthetic sodium fluorides being added to municipal water supplies and some beverages and foods are actually industrial waste products of the nuclear, aluminum, and phosphate fertilizer industries.

This is not new knowledge. A scientific study published in 1934 in the Journal of Industrial Engineering and Chemistry (Comparative Toxicity of Fluorine Compounds) revealed that industrial waste sodium fluorides are 85 times more toxic than naturally occurring calcium fluoride.

The Fluoride Health Hazard

Approximately 2/3 of the water supply in the USA now contains sodium fluoride. The addition of sodium fluoride to water and food creates additional serious health problems.

Researchers have linked long term daily intake of sodium fluoride with cancer, thyroid disruptions, a lowered IQ, Alzheimer's Disease, and disrupted melatonin production.

Most fluoride entering the body accumulates in bones and teeth. The damage to teeth from daily dental fluoridation has long been documented.

The Pineal Gland Impact

In the late 1990's British scientist Jennifer Luke was the first to study the effects of sodium fluoride on the pineal gland. Luke found that the pineal gland absorbs more fluoride than any other part in the body, including bones and teeth.

Cleansing Your Pineal Gland

Cleansing your pineal gland is important for those who wish to develop their multidimensional perception. The pineal gland naturally makes its own DMT when fully operational. Decalcifying your pineal gland is important to activate the pineal gland and awaken your third eye.

STEP 1 – The first step is to correct or eliminate any lifestyle habits which contribute to calcification of your pineal gland.

Calcium Supplements. Calcium supplements are a major causes of calcification. Get your calcium from natural organic foods.

Mercury. Mercury is also very bad for the pineal gland. Mercury tooth fillings are pineal toxins and should be removed.

Be careful eating fish and bottom feeders like shrimps and prawns. Tuna and dolphin flesh also contains higher doses of mercury. Generally speaking, the bigger the fish, the higher the concentration of mercury in its tissues. Mercury can be removed from the body by the daily ingestion of chlorella, wheatgrass or spirulina.

Non-Organic Fruit and Vegetables. Many pesticides are pineal toxins, so foods grown using these pesticides should be avoided. Fresh organic food is recommended. Organic healthy food with a high ratio of raw foods supports pineal detoxification.

Other toxins. Other toxins include artificial sweeteners such as aspartame AND/refined sugar, deodorants, cleaning chemicals, dental mouthwashes and air fresheners.

Toothpaste and Water. Sodium fluoride is present in toothpaste and most municipal tap water. It is magnetically attracted to the pineal gland where it forms damaging calcium phosphate crystals. Switch to a fluoride-free toothpaste and drink spring or filtered water.

The simple water filters you can buy in supermarkets do not take the fluoride out. Only reverse osmosis or water distillation will work. Fluoride can be removed from tap water with home reverse osmosis devices installed under a kitchen sink. You can also fill large jugs with water from reverse osmosis machines in health food stores and many supermarkets.

STEP 2 – There are a number of approaches you can use to decalcify your pineal gland, including those listed below:

Boron. Boron is a detoxifier and pineal gland cleanser and fluoride remover. It is best consumed by eating organic beets, or by mixing beet powder with spring water or other liquids or foods.

Garlic. Garlic dissolves calcium, acts as an antibiotic, and boosts your immune system. Consume half a bulb to two bulbs daily.

Iodine. Iodine is clinically proven to remove sodium fluoride via the urine. Most diets are deficient in this vital mineral. Eat seaweed foods and iodine supplements that combine iodine and potassium iodide.

MSM. This natural supplement is very powerful for general detoxification and is also good for hair, skin, nails and bones.

Oregano Oil. Oregano oil is a natural antibiotic against the calcium shells that nanobacteria form in the pineal gland.

Raw Cacao. Raw cacao is a great pineal gland detoxifier in high doses because of the high antioxidant content. It is also good as a pineal gland stimulant and can help activate your third eye.

Raw Apple Cider Vinegar. This is very good for the detoxification of your pineal gland, as it contains malic acid. Be sure that your vinegar is organic.

Sunshine. Frequent 20 minutes exposure to outdoor sunshine will help stimulate a pineal gland that has been calcified.

Tamarind. The pulp, bark and leaves of the Tamarind tree are used to make teas, extracts and tinctures that help eliminate fluorides through the urine. These are often widely used in Ayurvedic Medicine

Vitamins K1/K2. Very potent detoxifiers, especially when mixed with Vitamin A and D3. Can reverse arteriosclerosis and restore one's enzymatic balance. These remove calcium from the arteries and the pineal gland and properly store it in the bones, where it belongs.

These vitamins occur naturally: K1 (phylloquinone) is found in green leafy vegetables. K2 (menaquinones) is naturally created by intestinal microflora and also found in organ meats, liver, egg yolks, fermented dairy products such as cheese and butter, Japanese fermented soybean Natto, sauerkraut, shellfish, marine oils and fish eggs.

ELEVEN. RELATED RESOURCES

A Great Next Step...

Are you SERIOUS about activating your pineal gland to open your third eye? The author is a world renowned neuro-psychologist and 45-year pioneer in brain/mind research, and has helped people from around the world achieve higher states of awareness and consciousness.

This unique collection of downloadable MP3 special brainwave trainings will help you activate your pineal gland and experience third eye opening. This special collection of stereo-quality MP3s is valued at $52.80, but is only $19.95 for you, as a book buyer. You can get it here=>

http://QuantumLeapAudios.com/

Dr. Jill Ammon-Wexler

Ready to Go Deeper?

Are **YOU** one of those special people with a passionate desire to accomplish more in your life? If so ... Dr. Jill would like to personally invite you to come participate in her unique **QUANTUM MIND TRAINING PROGRAM**. Develop and refine your brain/mind power in the comfort of your own home. This exciting and unique 3-month online program is packed with training audios, videos, and brainwave training.

The end results include greatly increased creativity, focus, intelligence, total stress management, mental clarity, and remarkably superior levels of brain/mind performance.

Open up your natural genius and tap into higher, more valuable states of awareness and consciousness. Go learn more and take advantage of your book buyer's deep discount=>

http://www.HotBrainz.com

More......

Dr. Ammon-Wexler has written and produced a long list of books, ebooks, audiobooks and training programs. You can inspect these and read her latest articles here=>

http://www.BuildMindPower.com

Dr. Jill Ammon-Wexler

TWELVE. ABOUT THE AUTHOR

Author Jill Ammon-Wexler is doctor of psychology, dedicated metaphysician, and 48-year pioneer brain/mind researcher. She is also a "life adventurer" with a passion for finding, and then pushing beyond, her personal "limits."

She has pursued higher states of consciousness since her late teen years, first climbed a mountain alone at age 16, and then had to find her way down the mountain in a wild snow storm.

She also became lost several times in the deeply hidden wildernesses of California, navigating out by the stars. Over the years she was chased by a white shark, and went eye-to-eye with a wild mountain lion (on purpose).

During her university years she studied with amazing leaders like Fritz Perls, Virginia Satir, Soygal Rinpoche and Alan Watts. She also walked on fire, did sweat lodges, studied with shamanic elders, and become the holder of a coyote talking stick.

After receiving her Masters degree in psychology, she shaved her head and spent 6 months in a monastic Buddhist retreat. She then completed a PhD in psychology, became a clinical hypnotherapist and certified clinical biofeedback provider, and began her professional career as a pioneer mind power trainer and personal transformation coach.

Over the years Dr. Jill has also provided mind power training for organizations and individuals from around the world. She was also asked to provide support to ex-President Jimmy Carter's Special Commission on Women in Business.

Information about Dr. Jill's other mind-expanding books and training programs can be found at: **http://www.BuildMindPower.com**

REFERENCES

A 9-minute video of the results of third eye opening through meditation: http://tinyurl.com/8n8h4ol

----

ABC Science Online, 12 July 2006.
http://tinyurl.com/ftjag

Additional information about Huna symbols can be found here: http://tinyurl.com/97pzcb

Ammon-Wexler, J. Gamma through Delta brainwave training and its effects: http://www.hotbrainz,com

Ancient Hawaiian Huna methods are often taught at the Nine Gates Mystery School in California. Inquire here: http://www.ninegates.org/

Anodea, J. Eastern Body Western Mind: Psychology and The Chakra System As A Path To The Self. Berkeley, California, USA: Celestial Arts Publishing: 1996.

Axelrod, J. "The pineal gland". Endeavour 29 (108):1970.

Cunningham, P.M. Acupuncture Points: A Practical Guide to Classical and Modern Usage. Medford, MA. : 2000.

Davidson, R.J., Harrington A., eds. Visions of Compassion: Western Scientists and Tibetan Buddhists Examine Human Nature. New York: Oxford University Press USA: 2001.

Descartes R. Treatise of Man. New York: Prometheus Books: 2003.

Emerson, B. Self-Healing Reiki: Freeing the Symbols, Attunements, and Techniques. Frog Books: 2001.

Fuerstein. G. Encyclopedic Dictionary of Yoga. Paragon House NY, 1990.

Griffiths, R.R., Richards, W.A., McCann, U., Jesse, R. "Psilocybin can occasion mystical-type experiences having substantial and sustained personal meaning and spiritual significance." (PDF). Psychopharmacology 187(3):268-83. 2006.

Hunt, V.H. The Human Energy Field and Health: Scientific validation of the healing energies of "chi" and "prana." DVD available at http://www.malipupublishing.com

Jacobson, E. Progressive Relaxation. Chicago: University of Chicago Press: 1938.

Khanna, M. Yantra: The Tantric Symbol of Cosmic Unity. Inner Traditions: 2003.

Litscher, G. MDsc. "Shenting and Yintang: Quantification Of Cerebral Effects Of Acupressure, Manual Acupuncture, and Laserneedle Acupuncture Using High-Tech Neuromonitoring Methods." Medical Acupuncture: 2005.

Lynn, S.J., Judith W. Rhue, J.W. Theories of Hypnosis: Current Models and Perspectives. Guilford Press: 1991.

Ma, K.-W. "The roots and development of Chinese acupuncture: from prehistory to early 20th century." Acupuncture in Medicine 10:92–9: \1992.

Macchi M., Bruce J. "Human pineal physiology and functional significance of melatonin." Front Neuroendocrinol : 25 (3-4).

Marrone, R. D., Ed. Body of Knowledge, State University of New York Press: 1991.

Moore R.Y., Heller A., Wurtman R.J., Axelrod J. "Visual pathway mediating pineal response to environmental light." Science 1967;155(759):220–3.

Morey, G.K. Mystic Americanism. Kessinger Publishing: 2003.

Motoyama, H. Theories of the Chakras: Bridge to Higher Consciousness. Quest Books: 1982.

Nichols, D. In Psychopharmacology, Volume 187, Number 3, August 2006

Om. If you are not familiar with the OM or AUM sound, here is a free audio you can either listen to, or download: http://mp3.tamilwire.com/chanting-om-vinayagar-murugan.html

Phillips, S. Extrasensory Perception of Quarks. Wheaton, Illinois, USA: Theosophical Publishing House: 1980.

Rampa, L. The Third Eye. Ballantine Books: 1986.

Shri Anandi Ma is located at the Antioch, California Dhyanyoga Center. For information on teachings and Shaktipat Initiation, go to=> http://dyc.org/

Sieczka, H.G. Chakra Breathing. Mendocino, CA, Life-Rhythm: 1994.

Strassman, R. DMT: The Spirit Molecule: A Doctor's Revolutionary Research into the Biology of Near-Death and Mystical Experiences, 320 pages, Park Street Press: 2001.

Strassman, R., Wojtowicz, S., Luna, L.E., Frecska, E., Inner Paths to Outer Space: Journeys to Alien Worlds through Psychedelics and Other Spiritual Technologies. Park Street Press: 2008.

Strassman, S., "Hallucinogens" (chapter), in Mind-Altering Drugs: The Science Of Subjective Experience, Oxford University Press,: 2005.

Tapping expert Carol Tuttle on tapping your third eye chakra: http://thecarolblog.com/tapping-in-your-positive-feelings/

Tapping to clear your chakras – great video and ebook: http://tinyurl.com/2lyrmp

Printed in Great Britain
by Amazon